Dan Nolan – Missing
Based on a True Story

by Mark Wheeller

dbda

Dan Nolan – Missing
Based on a True Story

by Mark Wheeller

using the words of Daniel's family, friends and the detective in charge of the ongoing investigation.

Author's acknowledgments:

Pauline, Greg and Clare Nolan; DS Stewart (Hampshire Police); "Andy", George, "Jo", Sarah, "Thom" and their families, for giving me their words and permission to re-tell this story.
The cast of the Oaklands Youth Theatre production 2002/3.
The Dan Nolan – Missing Fund.
Meg Davis and all at MBA for their continued support and belief.
Evie, Dawn & Bharti from dbda who are always so willing to consider my plays for publication… thanks… and who pulled all the stops out to get this released VERY quickly.
My wife, Rachel, and children (Ollie, Charlie & Daisy) for love and support… and tolerance of long working hours.
Roy Nevitt (Stantonbury Campus) in the early eighties for his inspiration in the use of documentary theatre… "Dig where you stand".

Photographs: Nolan Family collection (page 8) and Mark Harbord (page 12).
Cover design: Based on that by Danny Sturrock for the original OYT production.

Published by **dbda** 2003. First edition.

ISBN 1 902843 10 X

BRITISH LIBRARY CATALOGUING IN PUBLICATION DATA
A catalogue record for this book is available from the British Library.

© Mark Wheeller 2003.
Copyright is strictly reserved.
The moral right of the author has been asserted.

No part of this publication may be transmitted, stored in a retrieval system or reproduced in any form or by means electronic, mechanical, photocopying, typescript, recording or otherwise, without prior permission of the copyright owner.
Photocopying of scripts is illegal! Even if you hold a licence from the Copyright Licensing Agency you are only allowed to photocopy up to a total of 5% of the whole script. Please remember the writers who depend upon their share of your purchases… without them the plays which you perform could not have been written or published.

Part of the proceeds from the sales of this book are donated
by the author to the 'Find Dan Nolan Fund'.

Further copies of this publication can be purchased from:
dbda, Pin Point, 1-2 Rosslyn Crescent, Harrow HA1 2SB.
Tel: 0870 333 7771   Fax: 0870 333 7772   E-mail: info@dbda.co.uk

Other Plays by Mark Wheeller

Chunnel of Love
Script: Graham Cole & Mark Wheeller
Duration: 100 mins
Cast: 25 (11f, 8m & 6m/f)

A bi-lingual play (80% English & 20% French) about teenage pregnancy. Lucy is fourteen - she hopes to become a vet and is working hard to gain good grades in her GCSE exams, when she discovers she is pregnant. She faces a series of major decisions, not least of which is what to tell the father... Ideal as a school production and Key Stage 4 Drama course book.

Sweet FA !
Script: Mark Wheeller
Duration: 45 mins plus interval
Cast: 3f / 2m (or more)
Published by: SchoolPlay Productions Ltd. Tel: 01206 540111

A Zigger Zagger for girls (and boys)! A new play (also available as a full length Musical) telling the true life story of Southampton girl footballer Sarah Stanbury (Sedge) whose ambition is to play Football (Soccer) for England. Her dad is delighted ... her mum disapproves strongly! An ideal GCSE production and Key Stage 4 Drama course book. Drama GCSE scheme of work also available.

Blackout – One Evacuee in Thousands   MUSICAL
Script: Mark Wheeller with the Stantonbury Youth Theatre
Music: Mark Wheeller
Duration: 90 mins plus interval
Published by: SchoolPlay Productions Ltd.

A Musical about the plight of Rachel Eagle, a fictional evacuee in World War II. Rachel's parents are determined that the war will not split the family up. After refusing to have her evacuated in 1939 they decide to do so midway though 1940. At first Rachel does not settle but, after the death of her mother, she becomes increasingly at home with her billets in Northamptonshire. When her father requests that she return she wants to stay where she feels at home. An ideal large scale school production with good parts for girls (and boys).

The Most Absurd Xmas (Promenade?) Musical in the World...Ever!
Script: Lyndsey Adams, Michael Johnston, Stuart White & Mark Wheeller
Cast: Big!
Music: James Holmes
Duration: 100 mins
Published by: SchoolPlay Productions Ltd. Tel: 01206 540111

Eat your heart out Ionesco! If you want a musical with a message ... don't consider this one! Santa fails to arrive one year in the Bower of Bliss. Why not? A shortage of carrots perhaps? Or is it because the central character is forbidden to use her musical gift, and whose parents disguise her as a cactus? It all ends reasonably happily and is a bundle of laughs. Originally conceived as a Promenade production. An ideal large scale school Christmas production or alternative an "absurd" summer production.

For more details and an up-to-date list of plays, please visit Mark's website:
www.amdram.co.uk/wheellerplays *(please note wheeller has two "l")*

All enquiries regarding performing rights should be made to: Meg Davis, MBA Literary Agents, 62 Grafton Way, London W1P 5LD. Tel: 020 7387 2076. E-mail: meg@mbalit.co.uk

Extracts from 'Graham – World's Fastest Blind Runner'

Graham:	Nothing was real to me until I'd touched it. That posed a problem... not everything I wanted to feel was easily examined by a small boy. One example, is something that sighted people take for granted... light. The best way for me to experience it was to touch it... so with the kind of precision demonstrated by the Dam busters *(Perhaps here the Dam busters music could be used and all, as aeroplanes, get into position!)*, Susan took me into our narrow hallway and lined me up underneath the lampshade hanging from the ceiling. There was little point in me touching it unless it was switched on... so...
Susan:	I clicked the switch... and he was off!
Graham:	With one foot on the wall I inched my way up towards the ceiling until I could feel the warmth of the bulb on my face...
Susan:	... then, like Columbus landing on America, he touched the "light".
Graham:	Owwwww!
Susan:	The joy of discovery was tempered by pain...
Graham:	... not just from the bulb!
Maud:	His shoes had been muddy... *(Maud smacks his backside)* ... my walls had been very clean.
Graham:	*(Holding his backside.)*... and my path to en"light"enment had to lie low for a few days while mum cleaned up my quest for illumination!

....

Roger:	The sun was blazing down on Varna Stadium.
Marie:	Graham and Roger climbed to the back of the stands to find some shade.
John:	In 90 minutes Graham would know whether all the hard work would be rewarded.
Graham:	My legs still felt sore from the previous evening's semi-finals.
Marie:	He stretched out on a bench and tried to relax.
Roger:	We could hear the flags flapping in the wind and a buzz of conversation amongst the competitors and the spectators.
Mark:	Thoughts came flooding into Graham's mind with no rhyme nor reason. *(Possibly the cast could create still images depicting the events as they are described to animate the thoughts.)*
Maud:	Unconnected incidents... like, how as a child he had ridden his bike in Woodland Street.
Marie:	How in his youth he had dreamt of finding fame and fortune as a rock star.
John:	His meeting with Ron Murray, and that great night at Crystal Palace when he became the first blind person to run on equal terms against sighted athletes.
Marie:	On hearing that his name was to appear in *The Guinness Book Of Records* for his world record run.
Roger:	He thought of his friends at home...
Marie:	His mum and dad...
Graham:	I stood up to cheer Bob Matthews home in the 1500.
Roger:	Are you ready?

Mark Wheeller's

GRAHAM
World's Fastest Blind Runner!

A play telling the amazing true life story of World Champion Blind Athlete Graham Salmon MBE who sadly died in 1999. It was premiered at the 2002 Edinburgh Festival Fringe.

"I came to know Graham Salmon in 1982 when, with Epping Youth Theatre, I wrote a play telling about his inspiring life. We became close friends. In 1998 Graham suffered an unbelievably cruel twist of fate. A malignant tumour was discovered in his leg... it had to be amputated.

Shortly afterwards my seven year old son, Charlie, asked Graham if he would join him in a game of football. I was concerned by this request but Graham had no such worries and took Charlie outside and played football with him... taking shots with his remaining leg and, as he became tired, used his crutch and did some headers!

It is for me the most "personal" play I think I shall ever write. Graham's life story is actually full of humour. The role of Graham provides an excellent opportunity for any actor. Most of my plays have been performed (brilliantly) by young people, adults in amateur companies and professional actors. I hope that GRAHAM will be embraced with equal enthusiasm."

Mark Wheeller

"Graham Salmon is the most inspiring athlete I have met; I say this without a moments hesitation even though I have enjoyed the rare privilege of sharing the company of Muhammad Ali, Stanley Matthews, Gary Sobers, Martina Navratilova, Nadia Comaneci, Arnold Palmer and countless others in the course of my job."

Robert Philip, Daily Telegraph

"I was really wowed by "Graham"... offered excellent opportunities for imaginative stylised performance with GCSE students... The peaks of tension and moments of pathos really moved me... I will definitely be offering 'Graham' to my classes this year.'

Neil Phillips, Head of Drama and Edexcel GCSE Examiner

"Very moving, very very funny, very well performed, very good!"

Bruce Henderson, Principal Teacher of Drama, Wester Hailes Education Centre, Edinburgh

GRAHAM – World's Fastest Blind Runner
ISBN 1 902843 09 6

Cast: 5m & 4f with doubling, or up to 34   **Duration:** 80 minutes   **KS 3/4 to adult**

Price: £ 5.50 per book / £70.00 for a set of 15

Wacky Soap - a 'gutsy' Musical to entertain and make them think...

Wacky Soap is a Pythonesque allegorical tale about drug abuse (also applies to alcohol or tobacco). While washing with Wacky Soap leads to instant happiness and an inclination towards outrageous behaviour, prolonged use washes away limbs and ultimately leads to dematerialisation. This has become a tried and tested (and increasingly popular) School/Drama Club/Youth Theatre production and is an ideal vehicle for a cast of any age.

'This (play) gave every member of the large and energetic cast opportunities to shine... King Huff addressed his subjects from a Bouncy Castle, just one of the touches of visual humour in this fast, funny and thought provoking evening'.
  Barbara Hart, Southern Evening Echo, Curtain Call Nominated "Best Production 2000"

Wacky Soap

ISBN 1 902843 02 9
KS 3/4 to adult
Duration: 50 mins play / 80 mins musical
Cast: 6-100!
Includes follow-up work for KS 3/4.
Price:
£ 4.95 per book / £65.00 for a set of 15

Wacky Soap The Music Score

ISBN 1 902843 06 1
A companion book containing the **Music Score** for all songs in the play and a **Mini-Musical** version for Junior Schools.
KS 3 & 4
Duration: 40 mins
Price:
£ 4.95 per book / £65.00 for a set of 15

A past performance CD gives you the opportunity to hear the songs of the play.
Price:
£15.00 each

Also available is a fully orchestrated backing track CD.
Price:
£25.00 each

The Story of **WACKY SOAP** A Cautionary Tale

ISBN 1 902843 07 X
A fully illustrated book with the story of Wacky Soap in narrative form. It serves as an ideal (and quick) way of introducing the scheme of work, included in the full script.
Price:
£ 6.95 per book / **£90.00 for a set of 15**

Dear Mark,
'Wacky Soap' was an outstanding success!!! We had a great deal of fun doing the show and we're still laughing... to quote our Head Teacher... 'the best school show I have ever seen'. We have had letters from people in the audience saying what a fab show it was and how impressed they were. The most frequent comment was that it was a 'risk' to put it on as a school show (as opposed to doing 'Oliver' or 'Little Shop of Horrors') and one that thoroughly paid off!! 'The feel good factor was amazing' was another comment we had. Many people said how impressed they were by the 'community' spirit of the production - everybody working together without the 'star' element creeping in!
So thank you - it has given us a huge boost!!
  John Plant, Head of Drama, Southmoor School, Sunderland

Other Plays by Mark Wheeller published by *dbda*

Too Much Punch for Judy

Cast: 2m & 2f with doubling, or 3f, 3m & 6   **Duration:** 35 minutes
KS 4 to adult

A hard-hitting documentary play, based on a tragic drink-drive accident that results in the death of Jo, front seat passenger. The driver, her sister Judy, escapes unhurt (or has she?). This play has become one of the most frequently performed plays ever!

'The play will have an impact on young people or adults. It will provoke discussion. It stimulates and wants you to cry out for immediate social action and resolution.'

Henry Shankula - Addiction Research Foundation, Toronto

ISBN 1 902843 05 3   Price: £ 5.50 per book / £70.00 for a set of 15

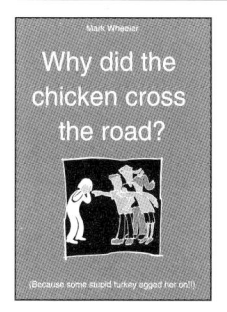

Why did the chicken cross the road?

Cast: 2m & 2f with doubling, or 3f, 3m & 3   **Duration:** 35 minutes
KS 3 & 4

The story of two cousins, Tammy and Chris. Tammy gets killed in a stupid game of 'Chicken' on the one morning that the cousins do not cycle to school. Chris, unable to tell anyone else about his part in the accident, has to live with this dreadful secret.

'An imaginative and moving look at risk taking at a time when peer pressure is at its strongest.

Rosie Welch, LARSOA

ISBN 1 902843 00 2   Price: £ 4.95 per book / £65.00 for a set of 15

Hard to Swallow

Cast: 3f & 2m with doubling, or 6f, 3m & 16   **Duration:** 70 minutes
KS 3 to adult

This play is an adaptation of Maureen Dunbar's award winning book (and film) **Catherine** which charts her daughter's uneven battle with Anorexia and the family's difficulties in coping with the illness.

'This play reaches moments of almost unbearable intensity... naturalistic scenes flow seamlessly into sequences of highly stylised theatre... such potent theatre!'

Vera Lustiq - The Independent

ISBN 1 902843 08 8   Price: £ 5.50 per book / £70.00 for a set of 15

Legal Weapon

Cast: 2m & 2f with doubling, or 1f, 3m & 13   **Duration:** 60 minutes
KS 4 to adult

A fictional story using oral testimony of RTA offenders and victim families, Legal Weapon tells the story of a young man's relationship with his girlfriend – and his car. Both are flawed, but his speeding causes the loss of a life and the loss of his freedom. Fast, funny and very powerful.

'To write in the language of late teenagers is a fine example of high artistic accomplishment.'

David Lippiett, Guild of Drama Adjudicators

ISBN 1 902843 01 0   Price: £ 5.50 per book / £70.00 for a set of 15

If you have enjoyed reading and/or working with this playscript, you may like to find out about other plays by Mark Wheeller. There are brief descriptions and other details on the following pages.

All plays are suitable for Youth Theatres, Schools, Colleges, and adult AmDram. They are ideal for GCSE Drama/English exam use and frequently do well in One Act Play Festivals. They offer both male and female performers with equally challenging opportunities.

All enquiries regarding performing rights should be made to:
Meg Davis, MBA Literary Agents, 62 Grafton Way, London W1P 5LD.
Tel: 020 7387 2076
E-mail: meg@mbalit.co.uk

For enquiries or to order plays published by *dbda*, please contact:
Bharti Bhikha or Manna Tailor, *dbda*, Pin Point, Rosslyn Crescent, Harrow HA1 2SB.
Tel: 0870 333 7771
Fax: 0870 333 7772
Email: info@dbda.co.uk

For Mark's other plays, please see details on the last page.

National Missing Persons Helpline

Early in 2002 Dan's parents contacted the National Missing Persons Helpline (NMPH) asking us to register him as a missing person and requesting our help. Since then NMPH has offered its support to the Nolan family as well as publicising Dan's disappearance in the hope of receiving information. Sadly, NMPH needs to provide this service to many families every day of the year.

It is estimated that annually over 200,000 people in this country go missing and about one third of these are young people aged under 16. The vast majority of these young people return within 48 hours, but others can disappear without trace for weeks, months or even years. Some people go missing by accident, some become the victims of crime, or even abduction – although this is the least likely.

The National Missing Persons Helpline was established as a charity in 1992 and handles over 100,000 telephone calls every year about missing people and young people who may have run away. We become involved in nearly 10,000 cases annually and have the most comprehensive database of missing persons in the country. The Helpline is a lifeline to many families, offering support, practical advice and help for as long as they need it.

The main threat to the Helpline's future is that it has become a victim of its own success. As its reputation grows and spreads, more and more people turn to it for help in seeking lost loved ones, which means ever-growing expense. NMPH relies solely upon donations to keep going.

If you should ever need help from NMPH then please call our **24 hour helpline on 0500 700 700**. For anyone who has left home or run away, and would like a message passed on to their family, please call our **confidential helpline Message Home on 0800 700 740**. If you would like to find out more about the work of NMPH, or about missing people, please visit our web site **www.missingpersons.org** or telephone us for an information pack on **020 8392 4545**.

NATIONAL MISSING PERSONS HELPLINE
(Registered Charity 1020419)

www.missingpersons.org

DANIEL

Daniel came into our lives when he was 8 years old, a sunny smiley face over the garden fence, once seen and never forgotten.

Over the years he has continued to run through our everyday life, sometimes in person and sometimes through the family and their justifiable pride in his many achievements, all of which he seemed to take in his stride.

Holidays are rare in this household but whenever we do manage to get away it is with the reassuring knowledge that our garden, along with the vast number of shrubs and plants in tubs will be carefully looked after by Dan, as are all the houseplants and most importantly the cat!

We shared in Dan's happiness when he won a scholarship to the King Edward VI School and more recently his sponsorship to university to be followed by a career in the Royal Navy. Daniel has always known what he wanted and worked hard to achieve it whilst retaining his sense of fun and his beautiful smile.

A VERY SPECIAL BOY

Annie Walton
Hamble

Some Letters

Dear Mrs Nolan,

A few lines to thank you so much for sending the poster of Dan. I now have it in the rear window of my car and pray that it will do some good.

As a mother of two teenage girls I can only imagine the torment and grief you must be experiencing, but I have to tell you we so admire your courage and positive attitude which inspires us to stay positive too.

Sarah had a very bad time during the first week and on her initial return to school, where I understand she sobbed throughout the first assembly. Now thankfully, although she still hangs on every word of the news programmes and scans the Echo, as we all do daily, she has managed to adopt a more positive attitude, which is much easier to deal with, and talks of when he comes back to school.

I hope it will be of some comfort to you to know that like many, many others we pray daily for Dan's safe return and also that you and all of your family are given strength to carry on.

Until that brighter day dawns, our love and best wishes to you all.

Sarah's Mum

About MateMinders

The Nolan family launched "MateMinders" in 2002, on Dan's 15th birthday. You can find more details about MateMinders on Dan's web site **www.dan-nolan.co.uk**.

Also there, you can find and download this A2 full colour poster.

Poster design courtesy of Pixel Scene Ltd.

Epilogue

(For printing in the programme, rather than performing.)

Pauline:	If you were in Hamble on the evening of 1st January 2002 and if you have not already done so, please come forward through the advertised phone lines or Dan's web site **www.dan-nolan.co.uk**.
Greg:	If you were in Hamble Village between 22:00 and 03:00 in the area between Hamble Motors and the foreshore.
Clare:	Any people leaving or removing their vehicles after 23:00 in either of Hamble's Public Car Parks (The Square, The Foreshore).
Pauline:	The two people seen in the Land Rover in The Square car park (opposite All Days) at around 23:30.
Clare:	The driver of a green van with white writing seen outside Barclays Bank at approx. 23:45.
Greg:	Anyone who was staying in Hamble that night, either with relatives or at one of the B&B's.
Pauline:	If you have any information to help in our search for Dan, no matter how trivial or irrelevant it may seem.
All:	We beg you to come forward.

Dan Nolan – Missing

Pauline:	We can't keep our kids locked up, they have to go out and explore, but safety in numbers is the only way to go in this day and age.
Greg:	Whether Daniel chose to leave his friends, or they chose to leave him is irrelevant…
Pauline:	"Now remember… there are weirdos about… keep your noses clean… and…
All:	… stick together."
FX Dan (with echo):	See you! Don't forget to save me some of that chocolate cake Mum.

Music 10: *My Darling Boy* by Sinead O'Connor.

The Stage darkens. The School Photo Missing Poster slide of Dan is illuminated.
The cast bow. The cast exit. The candle(s) on the cake continue to burn.

Section 7:   Mateminders

Pauline: If three teenage girls had been out that evening and had been drinking I wonder if they would have become separated. Girls are taught from a very young age about their vulnerability and are more acutely aware of staying together.

Greg: A girl would be nervous of being on her own at night, whereas a boy possibly doesn't think anything of it.
(Pauline moves to the Chocolate truffle cake and puts a candle in it. She lights the candle.)

Pauline: We used Dan's birthday in 2002 to launch Mateminders…

Greg: We want to find something constructive from what is every parent's worst nightmare…

Pauline: All this has to have happened for a reason… perhaps this is why…

Greg: We don't want anybody to feel how we are feeling.

Pauline: We need to try and make a difference.

Dan & Thom: Tonight's going to be a laugh!

Dan: Drinking…

Greg: … smoking…

Pauline: We've all done it… but if you do whatever it is together… you will be able to experiment more safely.

Dan: Shut-up and put the drink in my backpack before anyone sees it.

Pauline: The message we want to get across is to stay together all the time.

Greg: That was the golden rule… the only reason they were allowed out.

Thom: I looked back, but he wasn't there. I didn't think he could be that far behind.

Dan Nolan – Missing

Pauline: So many people walk such a fine line…

Greg: … and they survive.

Pauline: But what we do know is that IF Dan is dead…

Greg: Pauline… he isn't though…

Pauline: But you just said…

Greg: We can't talk like this…

Pauline: Greg, we've got to face it… if he is… we've been very privileged to've had a son like Dan… a very much loved son… who has brought us so much joy and laughter.

Greg: A son truly to be proud of

Pauline: We all miss him… we miss him dreadfully.

Section 6

Pauline:	I can't stop… just… trying to figure out what could have happened… every time there's a body found it's like…
Greg:	I know…
Pauline:	And it… it could go like this forever… But you know what really upsets me… it's that no-one was there with him. If someone had been there, it would almost certainly have reduced the chances of him being abducted. No one was there to raise the alarm. No one was there to witness it if he had gone in the river. No one was there to help him. He was on his own. That was probably the first mistake he had made… in his life…
Greg:	He was such a good lad… I don't mean goodie-goodie… I mean…
Pauline:	I know exactly what you mean…
Greg:	It's just not fair…
Pauline:	I want to… no I… I need to know what he went through… what he's going through…
Greg:	Pauline… there may never be a conclusion…
Pauline:	There's got be…
Greg:	We may never know what it is though… that's what I can't accept… can't get to grips with. *(Silence)*
Pauline:	Why Daniel? It doesn't seem real… it still doesn't seem real yet… yet…
Greg:	What?
Pauline:	*(Pauline composes herself.)* We'll never get over not knowing where Daniel is. *(Silence)*
Greg:	Life'll never be the same after all of this… even if he does come back… God I hope he does…

Dan Nolan – Missing

Pauline:	And frightened Dan
Dan:	Aaaaaargh!!!
M2 & F2:	*(Proud of Power)* So he turned and ran way
Dan:	Cos he was very, very frightened!
Pauline:	Conor believes he's somewhere on the grass verge on the Hamble Lane bend… Just a few yards from our house.
Dan:	He's waiting for a big gap in the traffic…
Pauline:	There's lots of cars on Hamble Lane…
M2 & F2:	He's got a mighty long wait!
Dan:	And when he thinks that there's about half an hour without any traffic…
F2:	He'll cross the road!!!
Dan, M2 & F2:	And make his way to our house.
Pauline:	*(This should be presented with much warmth and physical contact between the Nolan family and Dan… the reunion they dream of.)* When he gets within the four walls of our house, Conor has informed me, he will grow back onto his big size and he'll be fine then when he's inside… so I'll go along with that… I'm quite happy to go along with that.
Greg:	The children think about it… and so do we… it's with us twenty-four seven.
Pauline:	Greg… I was talking to this chap in Cowes today. *(Silence)* He lost his daughter. *(Silence)* It's a frightening thought. *(Silence)* Greg… he told me that kids in Eastern European Countries were being sold… sold for sex. Dan could have been abducted… he could have been down there… and gone aboard a boat or got in a car…
Greg:	Pauline… don't…

49

Section 6

Pauline:	I never dreamt in a million years that this far down the line I'd be no closer to finding him. Our lives have been changed for ever… our whole perspective of life has changed. It's been difficult for his brothers and sisters too.
Clare:	Tell them about what Conor said last night.
Pauline:	Oh yes… *(laughing)*… Dan's youngest brother has made up his own story of what's happened to Dan. It really made me smile. Last night he came down from his bed… he's going to kill me for saying this… he's decided that… since Dan's been missing he's been in…
	(Drumming begins. This scene should be presented in an energetic manner with the cast playing a variety of roles to animate the story imaginatively.)
All:	Africa.
M2:	*(Somehow becoming the camel)* On a Camel.
F2:	*(Directing the camel with Dan on top)* And he's recently made his way back to England.
Pauline:	However when he got close to Hamble…
	Slide 8: *School Photo Missing Poster.*
F2:	He became excruciatingly embarrassed by all of the publicity
Dan:	Aaaargh!!!
Pauline:	And he shrank…
M1:	… and he shrank…
F2:	… and he shrank…
Pauline:	Right down to a little person…
All:	Ahhhh!
Pauline:	Just as he arrived at our house a…
M2 & F2:	Great big giant came along.

Section 6: Aftermath

Pauline:	The night of the 2nd of January people in Hamble really wanted to do something to help…
Greg:	… they wanted to find him…
Pauline:	… a whisper went round the village… to meet up to do a search.
Clare:	700 people turned up… nearly a third of the population of Hamble.
Pauline:	We used that energy to make sure every area was covered.
Greg:	At least we knew Daniel wasn't lying in the undergrowth anywhere around here.
Pauline:	I was identifying items of clothing… anything at all that may have been his.
Clare:	The airfield search was hard… the grass is really tall so you have to shuffle your feet across to track the holes. I like saw my Grandad fall then get back up again. He went all the way across and all the way back again. He was so determined.
Pauline:	It was George who found bits of headlamp in a field 3-400 metres away from the pontoon.
Greg:	We phoned the police.
DS Stewart:	We've made an enquiry into that headlamp… it's inconclusive…
Pauline:	I am adamant that this was the one Dan had on that night… I know he'd lost another a few months previously… the inside of the battery casing and the spring on this battery terminal was still shiny. The blue plastic was clean. If it had been lying there for two months it wouldn't have stayed in that condition.
DS Stewart:	We hoped it'd have a unique serial number. Unfortunately it didn't. If it could be proved that this was the one he had that evening it would set up a whole new line of enquiry.

Section 5

Pauline: … not being caught on anything…

Greg: … not being shown up on the scanner would be virtually impossible… that's why we do not believe he is in the water.

Pauline: He had trainers on… they were never tied up.

Greg: If he'd fallen in…

Pauline: … he'd've kicked them off…

Greg: … instinctively.

Pauline: He had a woolly hat.

Greg: It would have been washed up.

Pauline: All the people who have fallen into the Solent since Dan went missing have turned up…

Greg: … most the next day…

Pauline: … they've all turned up. Recently the skipper of a boat, Chris Evans was on, went into the Solent.

Greg: He was recovered in a matter of hours.

Pauline: Water temperature and fat content of a person determines how long it takes a body to come up… if Dan hadn't got trapped he should've turned up quickly.

Greg: Four months is the longest any body has remained in that water.

DS Stewart: There is no evidence to suggest that Daniel has been abducted and no reason whatever to believe he has run away.
The police enquiry remains open.
(Exit)

Dan Nolan – Missing

Pauline:	There was a break in at a second hand clothing shop on the High Street. The only opportunity for that to have happened was on that night… the night Daniel went missing. He was wearing a £200 Henri Lloyd sailing jacket… now, if someone's going to break into a second hand clothing shop… *(A brutal [and very quick] murder on Dan is mimed)* what wouldn't people do for drug money?
Greg:	Perhaps he saw something he shouldn't have seen.
DS Stewart:	We've got the circumstances of the last time he was seen. What happened to him from that moment in time is a mystery. We are looking for something that says that Daniel is not in the water and is somewhere else.
Greg:	But we don't believe he went in the water…
Pauline & Greg:	… not at all.
Greg:	In the first three months that river was searched…
Pauline:	… every day…
Greg:	… on both tides…
Pauline:	All of the yachts there have been dived under… fingertip searches
Greg:	… so if he'd've got trapped,
Pauline & Greg:	… he would've been found.
Greg:	Two large sonar units have been on the river… army sonar units…
Pauline:	… and found nothing…
Greg:	… nothing. For Daniel to go in the river that night…
Pauline:	… to dodge every mooring line…
Greg:	… every boat…
Pauline:	… to get into the main channel…
Greg:	… to get out of the mouth of the river…

Section 5

Andy: As a parent you often wonder what your kids get up to when they are out on their own. But as kids go these four are probably the most reliable around, so, although it was cold on Jan 1st, the only requirement we made was they had to be back by 2.30am.
We never thought they would be taking a bottle of vodka with them. Yes Thom had tried alcohol before, he'd turn his nose at wine at Christmas, in fact he reacts to alcohol in the same way most kids would, with a look of disgust on his face. So to find 3 of the 4 had shared a bottle of vodka neat(!) was more than a surprise. I understand kids like to experiment with all sorts of things including alcohol. Unfortunately this experiment went very wrong… wrong in many areas. Dan and Thom were wrong to leave Jo alone on the bench when they went to the shop; Thom was wrong to leave Dan and walk back to Jo alone; and Jo and Thom were wrong to leave Dan to carry his own fishing stuff.
But, in my opinion, these wrongs happened because they had polished off a bottle of vodka. How can we expect one fifteen and two fourteen year-old boys to act normally after that? Without the vodka they always went together and came back together.
As I said before this was one experiment with tragic consequences. I know our loss is not the same league as Pauline & Greg's… it's not comparable… but… well… *(hesitantly)*… we can't avoid the feeling that… part of our Thom went missing too… on New Years Day 2002. *(Exit)*

Pauline: I find myself feeling guilty if I enjoy myself… feeling guilty about getting into a warm bed… feeling guilty about having a hot meal. To have one of your children missing is so hard… but life goes on… no… time goes on. Our lives are in suspension. There are so many unanswered questions… so many ideas of what might have happened…

Greg: But no evidence whatsoever.

Dan Nolan – Missing

(There is a slow motion movement sequence set to the music which leads to Dan "disappearing". It remains unclear where he has gone.)

Thom: When we got to the cutway I looked back to see Dan... but he wasn't there... I could see just up to where the corner bends away... but I didn't think he'd be that far behind. Jo went off to where he lives and I went back home.

Jo: In one word I'd describe Dan as "Quality".
Everyone knew Dan.
Since he's been missing Thom and me don't do as much things... when we make a joke there's always like...

Jo & Thom: ... one laugh missing.
(Jo exits)

Greg: The taxi driver sighted Dan's two friends but not Dan... even though he was looking out for his fare! The Nightwatchman... the one they call the Gaffa said he saw Dan's two friends leave the pontoon and go up past him. From where he was situated he should have had a good view of the pontoon.
It was a very bright night... but our Dan was never sighted. It's very, strange, very strange... like he vanished from the Victory to the pontoon... but people don't just vanish into thin air.

Thom: When Dan first disappeared I was very shocked. It didn't feel like he'd gone and no one knew where he was... it was more like he was on holiday or a school trip. It still feels pretty much the same... it's like I won't accept the fact that he has disappeared. As I think more and more about the things we did I'm starting to realise we won't be able to do them again... it wouldn't be the same. There are moments where I forget about it and think about calling for him... but I can't. There are so many things that I wish I could tell him... but I can't.
My dad wanted to... well... he just wanted to say something:

Section 5

Jo: I was feeling really rough... I lent up against a window...

Thom: You could say that I made the wrong choice in deciding to take Jo home... I didn't know who to go with.

DS Stewart: None of these boys were bad lads... just normal children.

Thom: I feel guilty about it... cos I could have... like gone down and helped Dan with his stuff.
(Thom shows through his movement the dilemma he is in. He veers towards Jo but remains looking at Dan. Greg moves into his path. Thom still looking towards Dan bumps into Greg prompting him to stop speaking. Thom backs off a little.)

Greg: It would only have taken a little while to go back down there and pack his stuff up...

Thom: *(Moving past Greg... but addressing him)*
... but I made that decision because I felt Jo was a lot worse off than Dan and anyway... he seemed to agree with what I was doing.

Jo: I just wanted to get home... as soon as I stood up again I thought I was going to be sick.

Thom: Dan said that he was going to follow us up.

DS Stewart: Witnesses talked about Daniel Nolan swaying around discussing the quantity of alcohol he'd drunk. Even considering an element of male bravado it becomes clear that Daniel played a significant part in his own destiny on January 1st 2002.

Greg: The alarm that Daniel had gone missing didn't go out for another 4 hours... vital time was wasted... because Daniel was on his own...

DS Stewart: Somewhere between the Victory Pub and the pontoon Daniel Nolan vanished.

Music 8: *Silent Night* by *Sinead O'Connor.*

Dan Nolan – Missing

Jo:	It's so frigging cold.
Thom:	A minute ago you said you weren't!
Jo:	That was a minute ago! *(He is struggling to pack his rod away.)* Oh my God!
Thom:	Come here I'll do that.
Jo:	Thom… I… I think I'm going to throw up again. *(He retches)*
Dan/DS Stewart:	Jo and Thom packed up their gear… and walked up into the High Street. They met Daniel Nolan outside the Victory Pub.
Jo:	My last image of Dan was coming down towards us… he seemed all right then. He could obviously hold his drink.
Greg:	At first, the police were told that this last sighting was on the bridge of the pontoon… placing Daniel much nearer the water. The facts of this last known sighting of our Dan… outside the Victory pub in Hamble at about 11:40pm were not established… until 4 weeks after Dan's disappearance.
Thom:	Dan, Jo's not feeling too good so I'm going to take him home.
Dan:	I'll come back as well. Can you help me with my stuff?"
Thom:	I've got Jo's…
Greg:	He had his and Jo's rods…
Dan:	OK
Thom:	All the time I was talking to Dan, Jo was walking on up the road… not very far but… I was like stuck in the middle…
DS Stewart:	Here were three boys, who had consumed a litre bottle of Vodka, which was nearly full, and one other caffeine type stimulant drink which would have increased the rush to the heart…

Section 5

Greg:	The lads at the bus stop told us that they asked Dan the time. He was able to read his analogue watch. It would appear from these comments that although he had been drinking he was still capable and aware.
Dan/DS Stewart:	Shortly after this the boys at the bus stop, realising the bus was not coming, get up and walk off. Daniel Nolan walks down the High Street towards the pontoon. He calls out to a woman who is parking a car. A party from the Bugle Pub walk up in the opposite direction. Another woman who knows Daniel drives down the high street and sees Daniel. He then walks to the top of the High Street and has a brief conversation with the Bugle party. His behaviour towards all of these witnesses leads the police to believe that Daniel Nolan was by any definition "drunk".
Thom:	*(To Jo on the Pontoon)* Jo… wake up mate… how are you feeling?
Jo:	A bit better.
Thom:	I'm freezing.
Jo:	I'm not… must be the vodka!!!
Thom:	What do you want to do then?
Jo:	*(Sitting up)* Where's Dan?
Thom:	He's met some people he knows up at the bus stop.
Jo:	*(Now feeling sick again)* Oh God!
Thom:	What?
Jo:	How long's he going to be?
Thom:	How do I know?
Jo:	Thom… I've got to get home… I'm feeling like… *(He retches)*
Thom:	All right. Let's pack our stuff up… then.

40

Dan Nolan – Missing

Thom:	I should have stayed so I'd've been with him… when they went home. We didn't see George's dad arrive… but after a while we went back down got on with our fishing. Dan'd caught three fish. We just sat there and talked… then Jo was sick… on the bridge.
Thom & Dan:	Bloody hell Jo!
Dan:	Are you OK?
Jo:	Does it look like it?
Thom:	Why don't you lie down and try and get some kip?
Jo:	*(Moving onto the bench)* I feel… phew!!!
Dan:	Thom… I'm off to get some chocolate.
Thom:	Will it still be open?
Dan:	Should be… it closes at eleven tonight.
Thom:	Jo's virtually asleep… is it alright if I come too?
Dan:	Will he be alright on his own?
Thom:	We'll only be a minute.
Dan:	Suppose… oh, come on then…
Thom:	I'll just wake him up and let him know… yeh?
Dan:	OK? Catch me up.
Thom:	Jo… Dan and me are just going up to the shop… is that OK?
Jo:	Fine… whatever. What's the time?
Thom:	Half ten.
Dan:	Come on Thom!
Thom:	The shop was shut but then Dan saw some lads he knew at the bus stop and went over to talk to them. I was getting cold, so I went back down to Jo.

Section 5

George:	He hasn't got a face…
Dan:	It's just cos the light's coming from behind him, you weirdo!
George:	Who'd wear a cloak like that these days? *(Jo & Thom come towards Dan & George)* Jo, Thom… have you seen that bloke?
Thom:	Who?
Dan:	The Gaffer. George thinks he's some kind of a… *(He does an impersonation of an Igor like character)*
Thom:	He's always there… he's alright.
Jo:	What's the time?
George:	Five to ten! My dad's going to be here in a minute…
Jo:	Where's the vodka?
Dan:	*(Dan takes the last swig from the vodka bottle)* All gone… anyway… you've had enough.
George:	I remember Dan hiding the bottle on a ferry. He didn't seem as bad as the other two, though he did have a few.
Thom:	He's strict your Dad… isn't he?
Dan:	*(To Thom & Jo)* If I were you I'd make yourself scarce… you don't want his dad to see you in that state… not unless you want everyone to find out what we've been up to.
Thom & Jo:	Back in a minute.
George:	When I left I turned to Dan and said: "See you later."
Dan:	See you mate…
George:	I left him there. *(George takes up a new position away from Dan)* Just the fact that I was there on that night when he went missing makes me think it was partly my fault. I could have told him to come home with me…

Dan Nolan – Missing

Dan: *(With a fish on his line)* Whoa… look at this one… what a beauty…

George: *(Looking in the opposite direction)* Dan?

Dan: George look! Brilliant eh?

George: Who's that?

Dan: Who's what?

George: Him up there. Creepy or what?

Dan: George… what are you talking about?

George: He's like someone off Scooby-Doo…

Dan: Oh him!

George: Do you know him then?

Dan: The Gaffa.

George: The what?

Dan: The Gaffer. If we mess about he chucks us off…

George: Seriously?

Dan: Yeh.

George: What about them two then?

Dan: They're alright… unless they come down here…

George: How do you know him?

Dan: I was here just before Christmas and he came right down…

George: What did he do?

Dan: *(Dan runs round George and pretends to draw a huge knife on him… then suddenly stops in his tracks.)* Nothing!
(He taps George on the head playfully)

George: He's creepy!

Dan: He's alright.

Section 5

George: I didn't have any.

Dan: Hey listen… whoever runs up to the pumps and comes back gets as much vodka as they can take.

Music 7: *One Fine Day* by *The Offspring*

All: *(Jo runs off to loud cheers from the others)* Go on then Jo… *(He returns) they all cheer and swig from the bottle. Music fades and underscores the remainder of the scene.*

George: As the night went on they got a bit more giggly. Jo and Thom started messing around… being high… talking out loud.

Thom: Jo and me were like…

Jo & Thom: *(Shouting form opposite sides of the stage)*… shouting at one another…

Thom: … nothing in particular… just larking about. *(They come together)*

George: They were falling on top of each other and acting as if they were drunk. One of them took some camouflage paint… green and black face paint… and put it on the other one.

Jo: Have some of this.

Thom: I'm covered… look… and it's on my coat!

George: They were up in the phone boxes pranking me… on my mobile.

Thom: *(On a mobile)* Have you caught any fish yet George? We went up to the phone boxes to call one of Jo's friends. *(They exit)*

George: Dan's Mum said later, that one girl who they were pranking was told by her mum to switch her phone off… cos they were being really rude.
They were totally out of it… well it seemed that way to me anyway.

Dan Nolan – Missing

Jo:	Dan?
Thom:	Couldn't you wait?
Dan:	I didn't have much!
Jo:	He'd drunk what would have filled the neck of the bottle.
Thom:	Tonight's going to be a real laugh…
Dan:	Maybe you'll actually catch a fish!
All 3:	Tell us the secret of your rod oh Mighty one!
Dan:	Shut up and put the drink in my backpack before anyone sees it.
	Music 6: *One Fine Day* by *The Offspring* *(plays loudly as the boys engage in a brief choreographed horseplay to establish the atmosphere of the evening and to represent the journey to the pontoon)*
George:	When we got down there we cast our rods out…
Jo:	The tide was coming in…
Thom:	… it'd be high tide at 12 o'clock.
Jo:	We were going to fish the tide in and then fish it out for a couple of hours.
Thom:	I don't tend to catch a lot…
George, Dan & Jo:	A lot? You've never caught anything at all! *(Dan catches a fish)*
Thom:	But Dan did all the time… don't ask me why.
George:	Dan and Thom had bought some stuff down to eat… Jo hadn't eaten since two o'clock…
Jo:	I wasn't really hungry
Thom:	Dan was drinking his milk
George:	And Thom was eating his nice cheesy Pringles.
Jo:	We thought the vodka would help keep us warm. *(He swigs from the bottle)*

Section 5: The Pontoon

Pauline:	From what George, Jo and Thom said and what Detective Superintendent Andy Stewart, in charge of the investigation has discovered, we've managed to piece together this version of what happened that evening: *(Dan enters wearing the clothes he wore on that night. He is rushing about to collect his stuff together.)* "Now remember… there are weirdos about so keep your noses clean… and stick together."
Dan:	*(Making to leave)* Don't forget to save me that chocolate cake Mum! *(Re-entering with fishing equipment)* Dan!
Thom (F2):	Thom!
George (M2):	George!
Jo (F1):	And Jo!
All:	Four boys… out for a night… and ready to… go!!! *(George runs off enthusiastically)*
Dan, Thom & Jo:	Not so fast George!
George:	Why?
Jo:	We've got to get something.
George:	What're you on about?
Thom:	Put your hand in the bush!
George:	Why?
Dan:	Go on… just do it…
George:	*(Bringing out a bottle of vodka)* Vodka?
Thom:	We were going to have it the night before last, then…
Thom & Jo:	Dan got grounded.
Dan:	Yeh… good one eh?
George:	It's been opened…
Thom:	Yeh and some bugger's nicked some…

Dan Nolan – Missing

(She moves, slowly, to a different position and settles)
After any holiday we're normally happy to be back with our friends, even though we're at school... but it was a very... I mean... everyone was trying hard to act normal... but it was... you didn't know what to... you didn't... know what to say... like do you talk about him in the past or in the present? Some people were saying that he'd been drinking... no one had that image of him... I was really surprised. I've never heard the Crush Hall be so quiet for an assembly... ever. Our priest said that we must pray for his family. It was the longest prayer we've ever had... there were a couple of sniffles in the audience... I was crying... a couple of people had to walk out. The whole place was so sombre.
That Maths book of Dan's that I borrowed... I've still got it... so it stays in my locker now... it's just a little memory of him, I wouldn't want to lose that.
Max was asked if he wanted Dan's stuff to be removed from his locker... he said; "No, he'll be back."
People hardly ever talk about Dan now... they say it upsets them. It's really depressing... it makes me think that if people aren't talking about him... they're kind of forgetting him.
I'll remember the little things... like him swinging on his chair or doing homework in the group bases... which the teachers say is forbidden... because homework, as the teachers say, is for home.
I'll remember his sense of humour and his smile...
I'll remember him making me laugh.
I won't ever forget Dan Nolan.

Music 5: *Dear Diary* by *Travis*.

Dan walks in slow motion across the stage. Sarah watches him. Intent on his journey he fails to notice her and leaves.

Section 4

Greg:	*(Comforting)* Paul.
Pauline:	He could be curled up in the undergrowth somewhere… and…
PLO:	I'm sorry Mrs Nolan.
Pauline:	*(Composing herself)* We'll need posters.
PLO:	I'll action that.
Pauline:	I'll get Dan's uncle on the case as well… *(To Audience)* thank God I did… We had to wait a good week before we had any from the police. Boys on bikes were knocking on the door and people took time off work to go out postering. They were going everywhere…
Greg:	*(To PLO)* We've also made a list of all the CCTV cameras in the area… could you check them out for us.
PLO:	Yes… thanks.
Pauline:	They didn't even know some of those cameras were there!
Greg:	It transpired that all of them were either broken or switched off!
Pauline:	People had heard it on the radio so we were getting loads of calls… but they thought it was Greg so I had to say, "No, it's Dan."
Greg:	Sarah, Dan's friend at school tells how she reacted to the news of Dan's disappearance:
Sarah (F2):	I knew nothing about it until the afternoon of January the 2nd. Mum was driving me home from dancing. The news came on… they said something like… a Hampshire boy has gone missing. Then… "Daniel Nolan". It seemed to be saying that he'd probably drowned… I was like… just speechless… my heart was pounding. One of _my_ friends. I felt like everything in my body had gone completely dead. It was a horrible feeling.

Dan Nolan – Missing

Greg:	… that Daniel's face would be absolutely everywhere, appeals on national TV…
Pauline:	… and everyone would be aware. We assumed that all the wheels just click into place and it just gets going.
Greg:	But it's not like that. There's no set formula as to what they should be doing… it's up to the individual police force…
Pauline:	It was almost like we were swept under the carpet… we didn't know how to handle that…
Greg:	… and we didn't know how to stop it.
Pauline:	I was horrified by the conversation we had, in our house with our first Police Liaison Officer *(Indicates PLO)* twelve hours after Dan went missing. The conversation went something like this… as I remember it.
PLO (Pauline's memory – M1):	I'm sorry Mrs Nolan. I really do think that you do have to accept that your son has slipped into the river.
Pauline:	*(Impassioned)* Why? Why? Did anybody see him?
Greg:	There's no proof whatsoever of anybody falling off the pontoon…
Pauline:	Is there any evidence?
PLO:	No.
Greg:	Who's saying this then?
Pauline:	Have you found anything at all?
PLO:	Well, no.
Pauline:	So he's missing, isn't he? You can't say he's drowned… he's missing. You're not looking for a stolen car… this is my son… my beautiful son… I'm not having assumptions made about him!

Section 4

	nightmare. I remember saying: *(Pause)* "Have I lost him?"
PLO:	Mrs Nolan… we mustn't jump to conclusions…
Greg:	… with it being slack high tide at midnight the chances were, that if Daniel had gone in the water… they'd find him… sooner rather than later.
Pauline:	At about half six in the morning I went to get some milk. It was a really eerie feeling because life was just going on as normal. When Dan's brothers and sister started to come round… I thought… how can I tell them?
Clare:	Mum what's going on?
Pauline:	I didn't want to wrap it up in cotton wool so I just said: "Dan went out fishing last night and hasn't come home."
Clare:	Oh God… I heard it on the radio but I… well I… Mum… where's he gone? He wouldn't…
Pauline:	Dad's out there looking for him.
Clare:	Mum… *(offering each other mutual comfort)* what's going to happen?
Pauline:	I don't know love… your dad's been out there all night.
Clare:	Haven't they found anything? *(Silence)*
Pauline:	Later that morning… I was down on the Quay and they were emptying the bins. I said: "You've got to check them first!"… they did when I was standing there but after that… I don't know.
Greg:	When an under 18 year old goes missing, an official body should move in. There should be set procedures.
Pauline:	We assumed that the police would take us through every step

Dan Nolan – Missing

Greg: I stayed down on the Pontoon for most of the night. It was quite slippery down there so my initial reaction was that he'd slipped in but there was nothing to say that, nothing at all… all his gear was neat and tidy…

He's been swimming in that river for years… and he wasn't the type of lad who panicked about anything. There's been instances out sailing where he's become trapped in the sails… quite serious situations and he's got out of them with no problem at all.

The tide couldn't have been calmer. It was the first high water. Although it was very cold, about -4°, if you'd put your hands in… it would feel warm… cos the water temperature is nine degrees higher. So, the initial shock, wouldn't have been that great… he'd've been straight back out again and anyway there's ladders both sides of the pontoon, and it's only 15-20 yards to the edge.

They had to do the search… they had to. Even though I was becoming more and more certain that he hadn't fallen in.

Pauline: *(On another part of the stage)*
I phoned the police.
They ask you questions… so many questions…

PLO (Pauline's memory - M1):   How old is he? What does he look like? Have you got any recent photographs?

Pauline: Their initial response was brilliant. By half past four all the emergency services were out on the water. The helicopter, the local Hamble rescue, dogs, police, you name it, it was out there…

PLO: Did he take anything with him… clothes… money?

Pauline: He'd taken nothing…

PLO: The money you said he'd saved for the holiday… could he have…

Pauline: We soon established that it lay untouched. It was a

Section 4

	walking past, going up towards yours.
Pauline:	Are you sure it was him?
Thom:	*(Silently nods his head in affirmation)*
Andy:	Pauline then phoned Jo's mum…
Greg:	… but there was no news…
Pauline:	Right… I'm going to phone the police. *(Exits)*
Greg:	When did you get back?
Andy:	About midnight wasn't it?
Thom:	*(Nods in affirmation)* He was just behind us.
Greg:	And you saw him going up our drive?
Thom:	I'm not sure…
Andy:	Thom… when did you last see Dan?
Greg:	He came home with you… at midnight?
Thom:	He wasn't with us exactly.
Andy:	So, after you got in you saw Dan going up his drive?
Thom:	*(Pause)* No.
Greg:	*(Pause)* You didn't?
Thom:	*(Pause)* No…
Andy:	Thom… what happened? Where is he?
Thom:	*(Pause)* I don't know. He followed us home… I know he did…
Greg:	This' looking serious… I'm going back to the pontoon. *(Makes to exit)*
Andy:	What do you want us to do? *(The Action freezes momentarily.)*
Pauline:	I phoned the police. I wasn't panicking… but it was just that I had to get the ball rolling… to get everything going.

Dan Nolan – Missing

Greg:	I'll go round... if he's not there... we'll have to call the police... but he will be... he's got to be...
Pauline:	What are you going to say? They're going to be devastated... what are you going to say Greg? *(Silence. Pauline and Greg move to an area representing Andy's house. They knock and call his name in a panicky manner... but with control over volume.)*
Andy (M1):	*(Wearing a dressing gown)* At four o'clock I was woken up with a panicky banging on the window. I had absolutely no idea who it was... having heard Thom come home I thought it can't be to do with the boys... so... I went to the door. Pauline was stood there, and her words were:
Pauline:	The boys aren't back from fishing.
Andy:	*(Bleary eyed)* My Thom's in.
Greg:	Is our Dan there?
Andy:	No.
Pauline:	Can you check?
Andy:	He's not there.
Pauline:	Can we talk to Thom?
Andy:	Thom came out to the top of the stairs.
Greg:	Do you know where our Dan is?
Thom (F2):	*(Wearing a dressing gown)* Isn't he at home?
Pauline:	No... he did come home with you, didn't he?
Thom:	He was following us...
Pauline:	I've just been down to the pontoon... his stuff's still there.
Thom:	He said he was going to come up behind us...
Greg:	Wasn't he with you then?
Thom:	We just... I don't know... when I got in I saw him

Section 4

	Greg… something's wrong. I'll go down there. *(She exits)*
Greg:	She flew down to the village… about five minutes away in the car… while I got dressed… I was up… pacing about and ready… just waiting for Pauline to come back…
Pauline:	They're not there… their stuff's all there… but they're not.
Greg:	Are you sure?
Pauline:	Course I'm sure.
Greg:	They must be.
Pauline:	They've fallen in…
Greg:	They can't have done…
Pauline:	I think they have… all their stuff's there… on the pontoon…
Greg:	What?
Pauline:	Dan's tripod stand was like collapsed in the corner… like he'd prepared to pack it away then suddenly stopped… or I don't know… been stopped… one of them must have fallen in and then…
Greg:	Pauline love…
Pauline:	His backpack was… like it had just been chucked down… it was in the middle…you had to go round it to get to his other stuff… and his gloves… they were there as well. It was really spooky. What are we going to do Greg? It just doesn't make sense.
Greg:	He's probably round one of his friends.
Pauline:	But they wouldn't leave their stuff on the pontoon?
Greg:	I'll go round to Thom's… *(To Audience)* Thom only lived two doors away.
Pauline:	What if they have fallen in Greg?

Section 4:   Missing!

Pauline: I woke up in the front room at about 10 past 2. Dan wouldn't want his mother sat on the couch waiting for him... so I went up to bed... and waited... expecting to hear him come up the stairs... you know... typical teenager... then stick his head round the door to say he's caught something or whatever... he always let me know that he'd got home safely.
Come half two, quarter to three it hadn't happened. I was in bed looking at the digital clock and I said to Greg:
"Dan's not home yet." I'll never forget Greg's words... "That's a bit cheeky." Not that's unusual... but...

Greg: That's a bit cheeky... I thought they'd've been home earlier tonight... cos it's cold.

Pauline: I'm going to find out what's going on.

Greg: Pauline, are you sure?

Pauline: He's not back!

Greg: He's probably round at one of his friends.

Pauline: Now, Dan doesn't have a mobile...

Greg: We say to our kids that we'll get them a mobile, but they have to pay for the calls.

Pauline: ... and although he's quite a little entrepreneur making quite a bit of money...

Greg: ... he's very thrifty and wouldn't spend it on phone calls.

Pauline: I rang both his friends and got their answer phones... I didn't want to disturb their parents as it was... well... they had work in the morning.

Greg: I was beginning to feel really uncomfortable.

Pauline: I remember, getting a glass of milk and thinking, "I don't want to go into panic mode and over-react... but I must do something!"

Section 3

Sarah:	Please.
Dan:	Fine… *(He gives the book to her. Dan Exits… Sarah watches him leave)*
Sarah:	The last time I saw him was on the final day of the Christmas term. We were in this hyper-small corridor at our lockers and everyone was coming past us… *(Max enters…)* piling in. *(Max is barged over by a friend)* Max, Dan's locker partner actually got pushed onto the floor. *(They help Max [M2] up.)* We were all in hysterics. As people gradually move off, you wish them a Happy Christmas. I was the last one… talking to my friend. Dan was walking out with Max and I just called out: "Bye Max… Bye Dan."
Max:	See you.
Dan:	Bye.
Sarah:	I remember them saying…
Max & Dan:	Have a good Christmas.
Sarah:	"Yeh… you too!" It was just a little moment. *(Pause)* I wish I could have said goodbye properly.

Music 4: *Humpty Dumpty Love Song by Travis.*

Daniel, in slow motion passes Sarah an item… perhaps the school blazer he was wearing for this scene. He gives her the item. She takes it. He leaves… perhaps she kisses him lightly, the "goodbye" she wished she was able to do… perhaps it is denied to her. Sarah watches him leave.

Section 3: Sarah's Story & That School Photograph

Pauline:	Shortly after Daniel went missing I received a lovely letter[3] from the mother of a girl, who knows Daniel at school saying how we've actually helped her daughter, Sarah *(Sarah enters wearing school blazer, as do the others in this scene),* who was with Dan when that school photo, we just showed you, was taken. It was the one we have ended up using in the 'Missing' campaign.
Sarah: (F2)	We went in one by one… they had a mirror just before you go through the curtain tab and I was looking at it… Dan and his mates were having a laugh… mocking us
Dan:	*(Overplayed with affected voice)* Does my hair look OK?
Max: (M2)	*(Overplayed with affected voice)* Does my make up look OK?
Dan:	*(Overplayed with affected voice)* Oh, can I borrow some lippy?
Sarah:	He was just making jokes… but my friend… she was having a fit about it…
Lorna: (F1)	*(Suitably over the top)* I so wasn't ready! They took the picture like this. *(She pulls a funny face and remains momentarily in a still image.)*
Sarah:	A little while after that I was at my locker and just couldn't find my Maths textbook. Dan was always last, and he was casually getting his stuff together… him so laid back… and me frantically searching… Oh, I'm going to get so told off! Dan, have you got your Maths book?
Dan:	Which? This one?
Sarah:	Yeh…
Dan:	Do you want to borrow mine?

---

[3] *See copy of Sarah's Mum Letter on page 56.*

Section 2

Greg: A local newspaper wrote an article about one of the searches, after Dan had gone missing.

Pauline: Before we'd even seen it the newspaper concerned rang me up to apologise profusely.

Clare: Next to the article was a picture of Dan with the caption underneath…

Slide 5 – Close up of Dan with Sadaam Hussein caption.

All 3: Sadaam Hussein!

Pauline: Bless them… they were horrified… but we just laughed… Dan would have really appreciated that.

Clare: He loves the water… swimming, sailing, fishing, canoeing, Sea Scouts…

Pauline: And he desperately wants to join the Royal Navy… as an Officer.

Slide 6 – Navy letter.

Greg: Four months after he vanished he was offered a place at the Royal Navy College in Dartmouth for a potential Officers Acquaint course.

Pauline: It was so sad… frustrating that Daniel wasn't here to take up this marvellous opportunity which he's initiated himself… hopefully he'll be back soon to contact them and take this further.

Slide 7 – Dan's School Photograph 2001.

Dan's such a switched on kid… he was awarded a bursary into King Edwards School in Southampton. He was involved in every possible club going from chess to football…

Clare: He was so proud of being the top scorer for his team for a while...

Greg: He was the anchor to our family.

Pauline: When he bought his school photograph home I remember I put it up against the first one he had done. He'd grown into a young man.

(The Water Music continues providing an aural bridge to the next section.)

Section 2: A Much Loved Son and Brother... Daniel

(During this showing of pictures slides are shown to the accompaniment of Adagio from Handel's Water Music)

Slide 1 – Dan as a baby [2].

Pauline: Daniel was born on the 5th February 1987 weighing in at 9lb 12oz.

Greg: His easygoing nature was soon shown by regularly sleeping 12 hours straight, at the tender age of just six weeks.

Pauline: This is Daniel at two months old, very bonnie baby, and already that smile, that everyone knows only too well, is developing. I wouldn't exactly say he's cute... more like a little chubby Sumo I suppose!

Slide 2 – Dan with Bass.

This one shows Daniel when he's about 5 years old... holding up proudly his first Bass...

Clare: A very big Bass...

Greg: He's holding it correctly with the fingers in the gills...

Pauline: ... again that smile's there and those dark eyes shining away. Daniel's a very keen fisherman... very keen. He and his Dad have a very, very special bonding between them over the fishing. Greg summed it up to me:

Greg: He's not just my son... he's my best mate.

Slide 3 – Dan and siblings.

Pauline: Dan's the eldest of 5. Eighteen months after Dan we had Clare, she's the only girl. Almost three years to the day we had Liam, the tiger of the family, then little Patrick came along, known to Dan and all of us as Pip. Then last, but certainly not least, and very much loved and...

Clare: Cheeky one of the family... gets away with everything.

Pauline: Is little Conor... so that's the Nolan family.

Slide 4 – Dan with Sadaam Hussein caption.

---

[2] *The slides referred to in this and other scenes are available for use in performances of the play only. For details contact Meg Davis, MBA Literary Agents Limited, 62 Grafton Way, London W1P 5LD. Tel: 020 7387 2076   Fax: 020 7387 2042   E-mail: meg@mbalit.co.uk*

Section 1

Clare: When mum falls asleep I always come down and I say: "Mum it's really uncomfortable down here… why don't you go to bed?" But she doesn't… she worries.

Music 3: *You're The One* by *The Carpenters*

Dan Nolan – Missing

	knocking over of a television. Speaking in slow-motion voices) Television.
Clare:	The telly got knocked over…
Pauline:	Greg was furious. *(M2 becomes Greg and looks at Dan sternly)*
Clare:	Dad made them all go out onto the back lawn and pick up the dog pooh… *(Dan mimes picking up a piece as though with his hands)*
Pauline:	*(To Dan)* We did actually give them a pooper-scooper thing. *(Dan corrects his mime with a laugh)* To look at them you wouldn't have thought it was punishment…
Clare:	They were all really laughing.
Greg:	His mates must have been really fed up with him when he was grounded… he messed up all their plans.
Clare:	Plans that none of us, at that time, were aware of…
Greg:	We didn't detect anything out of the ordinary.
Pauline:	We just had our dinner, cleared up… then watched **Shakespeare In Love**. Clare went straight up to bed afterwards…
Clare:	… which was quite early for me… night Mum.
Pauline:	Night. Greg had gone up earlier 'cos he was due back at work after the New Year break. I went to shut the computer off… it was half past eleven… I saw the clock on the computer. I was sat in the corner and I had a real wrenching feeling in my tummy… like all of my insides being pulled out. "Why am I feeling like this?" It was horrible. I wanted to go down to the quay… I shook it off thinking… "Pull yourself together Pauline… you'd be such an embarrassment for Dan". Then… I just fell asleep watching the telly…

Section 1

Pauline	It was about 8 o' clock. They left by the back door, laughing and joking. I went to put some rubbish out and noticed the light was on in the garage. The door was half open and Dan was ducked down under it. He had his backpack on and was getting some bait from the freezer out there. I can remember… by the bins… it's strange… I really took that moment in. I don't know why… but I remember standing there just looking at our Dan.
Clare:	I heard the gate going and glanced out of the window… and there was Dan… always with his head down… always going fishing… carrying loads of stuff, fishing rods, tripod stand and his bucket… this really big bucket… which I saw George take off him… like… to help *(Pause)* That was the last I saw of him. We were just starting to get close when he vanished… it was the worst timing.
Pauline:	And off they went… about a fifteen-minute steady walk… one was fifteen and the other three were coming up to fifteen and they were going fishing… they'd all been before… it was all so "normal".
	Music 2: *My Darling Child* by *Sinead O'Connor.* *(Dan repeats his departure in the manner described above… but in slow motion to the music. Pauline and Clare look on.)*
Clare:	They had actually planned this fishing trip two days earlier, on the 30th but Dan had been grounded so they couldn't go…
Pauline:	He'd been play fighting in the front room with his brothers… *(Dan enters with his brother Liam [M2] setting up a brief series of images accompanied by loud overstated vocal reactions to establish the cushion fight.)*
Clare:	They were really going for it…
Pauline:	Things got a bit out of hand and
Dan & Brother:	*(Miming in slow motion them trying to save the*

Dan Nolan – Missing

Dan:	Can I have some now?
Pauline:	No you can't!
Clare:	*(Entering)* He adored that chocolate thing…
Dan:	Save some for when I come in tonight… please!
Pauline:	We did… *(She places it on a table SL)*… but he was never to have it. *(Pause)* A few moments later Dan was sat on the couch with his Dad on one side and Clare on the other…
Greg:	He had two packs of… these noodley type things…
Clare:	Two great big packets!
Pauline:	Two huge great packets of…
All:	Super Noodles.
Greg:	Then the friends that he was going with came up the driveway…
Pauline:	Dan has lived in Hamble all his life. He has known George since Playschool and has known Jo and Thom since the middle of primary school. They'd played in the same football team… all palled up… they were always together… They were regular fixtures and fitting in our house… up until Dan's disappearance. They all stood there in a little line by the back door… the four of them…
Pauline/Greg:	Dan, Jo, Thom, & George…
Pauline:	… you know they were just leaving and I said to them: "Now remember… there are weirdos about so keep your noses clean… and stick together."
Greg:	That was the golden rule… the only reason they were allowed to go. "Stick together."… They were the last words she said to them.
Dan:	See you! *(Making to leave)* Don't forget to save me some of that chocolate cake Mum.

17

Section 1

Dan:	I'll get something else.
Pauline:	It's roast…
Dan:	Don't worry!
Pauline:	I had this sort of daydream the other day… Dan was at the door… and I didn't know what to do… I was thinking "Oh my god, who do I ring first to say that he's home?"… and Greg said:
Greg:	Just bring him in and give him a cup of tea!
Pauline:	There's a big emptiness in our lives.
Greg:	Some nipper came round this afternoon asking if you were doing another Fishing Competition.
Dan:	Who was it?
Greg:	Different from the one who came last week.
Dan:	How old… did Pip know him?
Greg:	Older, I think.
Dan:	What did you say?
Greg:	I said I wasn't sure… and what with exams and…
Dan:	Dad…
Greg:	I didn't know what to say…
Dan:	If anyone else comes, get their name and address and tell 'em that there will be another one… soon… OK… it was a laugh, and it made a bit of money.
Greg:	Sorry.
Pauline:	*(Entering with Chocolate Truffle cake)* Dan… look…
Dan:	What?
Pauline:	I'd got his favourite…
Dan & Pauline:	*(She holds it up for him to see)* Tesco's Finest Chocolate Truffle Cake.

Dan Nolan – Missing

Pauline:	It was like I didn't want to have the responsibility of making that decision. I remember getting something out of the fridge, Dan standing by the back door and I just delegated it… I said… "Ask your father."
Greg:	It's going to be a cold night…
Dan:	And?
Greg:	Just saying.
Dan:	Can I go then?
Greg:	What did Mum say?
Dan:	She told me to ask you.
Greg:	What time are you going to be back?
Dan:	2:30… at the latest.
Greg:	Fine by me.
Pauline:	We've never had any problems with Daniel being out late, he always arrives home on time. He's trustworthy, with friends and the pontoon's well lit… but criticism did come back after Daniel went missing:
All:	*(Changing role for a moment)* "Fancy them letting him out at that time of night!"
Pauline:	He'd been going fishing since he was little… the lads had been going night fishing over the last year… we were cool with it… no problems at all… you can't keep your child tied to your apron strings all your life.
Dan:	*(Reverting back and talking to Greg)* Can I take that bait we were going to use the day before yesterday?
Greg:	Course you can.
Pauline:	You're not going to have time for your dinner! Shall I put it up for you?

Section 1

Pauline:	*(To the audience, contrastingly slow paced)* All the clairvoyants I've spoken to say somebody took our Dan. One said he'll definitely come home. None have said he went in the water.
Clare:	We've kept Dan's light on since the day he vanished… it won't go off until he comes home.
Pauline:	We're not in denial… we're in hope. I wake up every day thinking we could get some vital information. However I realise it's probably just another day I've got to face.
Clare:	When I'm sitting by the door at school I play this game. I tell myself if I look up, the receptionist will be there to tell me my brother's returned home. It may be stupid but sometimes I do look up.
Pauline:	The other day a "head" was found in Basingstoke… straight away I thought… it's Dan… it was really scary. I don't know if this will come across properly but when they found Millie Dowler… your heart goes out for that family… but the thing that went through my mind was that they didn't have to wait any longer… it's almost like… like it's a conclusion. Our lives are evolving around the fact that Dan is missing. The 1st of January 2002 was "just another day"… but after all that's happened, I remember it so vividly. *(As the cast move into the live action the pace picks up.)*
Dan:	Mum?
Pauline:	Yeh.
Dan:	Can I go fishing?
Pauline:	What time will you be back?
Dan:	Twoish.
Pauline:	Ask your father.
Dan:	OK

Section 1: Noodles and out!

The Missing poster of Dan Nolan is illuminated.
SL is a stand on which the Truffle Cake will be put. On SR there is a small selection of Musical instruments, used during the play.

Music 1: *Silent Night* by *Sinead O'Connor* *plays* [1].
Thom, Jo, George and Dan enter and set up for some fishing. All are wearing clothes suitable for a cold night's fishing. Dan has a beige Henri Lloyd jacket, blue cotton trousers and Airforce blue DC's with the laces untied. The boys are lit as though by moonlight. They drink from a vodka bottle and as they do so the mood changes.
Music with a Skate Punk **(Blink 182 – All The Small Things)** *feel fades in underneath the Sinead song… Thom and Jo begin to mess around involving Dan and George in their japes… amongst other things they prank call to George's mobile and laugh. George leaves. Jo and Thom continue to lark around energetically. Finally Jo is sick. Thom helps Jo home… Dan remains on his own… the lights crossfade to establish a lighting state suggesting Dan's home. Dan begins to "headbang". Clare enters angrily.*

Clare:	*(Shouting over the music)* Turn it down Dan!
Dan:	*(Shouting over the music)* What?
Clare:	*(Shouting over the music)* Turn it down!
Dan:	*(The music stops)* That better is it?
Clare:	You're so selfish playing all that banging stuff so loud!
Dan:	Well I'm out tonight so you can play "Westlife" up full and prance around as much as you like!
Clare	We're a typical brother/sister… 18 months apart. *(Laughing)* We compete to see who can play the loudest music.
Dan:	*(Dan is getting his stuff together to go out)* No contest!
Clare:	He's got a better cd player than me so he always wins.

---

[1] *The songs/music suggested at various points in the play are suggestions only. Mechanical Performing rights are not included in any performing rights associated with the play and must be applied for, to the appropriate bodies separately.*

The Oaklands Youth Theatre Production

Left: The pontoon scene with Rachael Dennett (Thom) seated and Darren Harley (Dan) standing.

Above: Alex Chalk (Greg) with Darren Harley (Dan) and Rachael Dennett (Clare).

Left: Alex Chalk (Greg) & Kate Dean (Pauline).

Above: The 'head banging' scene with Rachael Dennett (Clare) and Darren Harley (Dan).

Dan Nolan – Missing

Dan Nolan – Missing was Premiered
by the Oaklands Youth Theatre
at Oaklands Community School Theatre
on Saturday 23rd November 2002
with the following cast:

Pauline Nolan/Jo	Kate Dean
Dan Nolan/DS Stewart/Andy	Darren Harley
Greg Nolan/George	Alex Chalk
Clare Nolan/Thom/Sarah	Rachael Dennett
Director	Mark Wheeller
Assistant Director & Lighting Designer	Danny Sturrock
Sound	Ollie Wheeller/Laura Clarke
Photography/slides	Mark (Sparky) Harbord
Live Music	Arjun Malhotra/Charlie Wheeller

Productions of ***Dan Nolan – Missing*** should use minimal props, costumes (with the exception of Dan who was kitted out in duplicate clothing) and setting so that the play can be performed without a break. There should be no blackouts and scene changes should be incorporated into the scenes or underscored with pre-recorded music.

List of Characters

The play was originally written for four actors although there are many more characters than that. Casting for four actors would be as shown opposite, in the cast listing for the Oaklands Youth Theatre production.

Dan Nolan – Missing can be performed by any number from 4 (2m/2f) to 20 (10m, 4f, 6 m/f).

Cast list in order of appearance

Dan Nolan	Fourteen year old. Needs to be dressed in a grey "Benny" hat and beige Henri Lloyd jacket… with blue trousers. Was wearing a red fleece under it.
George	Fourteen year old
Thom	Fifteen year old
Jo (male)	Fourteen year old
Clare Nolan	Dan's younger sister. Thirteen years old.
Pauline Nolan	Dan's Mother
Greg Nolan	Dan's Father
Liam Nolan	Dan's brother (in the dog pooh scene)
Sarah	Dan's school friend
Max	Dan's school friend
Lorna	Dan's school friend
Andy	Thom's father
Police Liaison Officer	As remembered by Pauline
DS Stewart	Detective in charge of the investigation
Conor Nolan	Dan's six year old brother
Chorus	Mostly in Conor's story

Dan Nolan – Missing

A note from Pauline and Greg Nolan

We have watched those desperate appeals on TV by parents whose children have gone missing, so many times it seems. "What a terrible situation, we could never cope if we lost one of our children!."

All natural reactions, never believing that we would ever be in this situation – but, here we are. Never believing that out of our five children it would happen to Dan, but it has.

Nobody is invisible. Life is very fragile. This can happen to anybody irrespective of class, nationality, religion or location. It is devastating to the friends and families who have to deal with a loved one being missing, the not knowing! We need to know where Dan is and this is why we were happy for Mark to write Dan's story in the form of this play.

We hope for two things: Firstly that the play will be seen by somebody who may have that vital missing link regarding Dan, therefore allowing us to locate his whereabouts. Secondly, to try and find something constructive from every parent's worst nightmare. We believe that all things happen for a reason. Maybe this is why Dan has gone missing?

> We don't want anybody to feel how we are feeling.
> We need to try to make a difference."
>
> *Pauline Nolan*

The school photo of Dan Nolan as used in so many of the posters the family have distributed in their 'Missing' campaign.

A substantial Reward (£50,000) is being offered by Dan's family for any information leading to his safe return. For full details please visit Dan's web site **www.dan-nolan.co.uk**.

Dan Nolan – Missing

The director should try to be imaginative and animate the scene to keep the visual interest for the audience as high as possible without detracting from the power of those "real" words.

All of us who were involved in the first production of the play have become passionately involved with the subject matter and hope that our efforts and those of other groups who also choose to present this play may help to solve the mystery of Dan's disappearance.

People often ask me what good do I think the play can do. One overwhelming answer to this (beyond the more obvious raising of issues) is that it can keep people talking about Dan Nolan. I have come to realise a massive tragedy behind this story which is really disturbing. If the Nolan family had remained silent following the tragic events of January 1st 2002, the public consciousness of Dan would have quickly faded. It is vital that we all keep talking about Dan, and try to get others talking about him too. The play will help in this respect... I am certain of this... and it takes as its inspiration the determination of his family.

It goes without saying but I will say it anyway... I hope something soon will come up that will help solve the tragic mystery surrounding Dan's disappearance. I look forward to meeting him... and I am keen to add to this play the reunion scene his family so much deserve.

Introduction

It gave that photo, in its original setting, an added poignancy. I remembered my own school photos that I had wanted to hide from other people... and wondered what Dan had thought of this one, little knowing how well known it was destined to become.

Immediately I realised that the Documentary style of writing I had used for **TOO MUCH PUNCH FOR JUDY** and **GRAHAM** was the only way in which this play could be written. It was important to convey the facts and opinions in the way that the people who had experienced this situation first hand phrased it. Consequently **DAN NOLAN – MISSING** uses the words of Daniel's family, friends (some of whom were with him that night) and the Detective in charge of the ongoing investigation, to try and get as close to the truth as memory will allow. On interviewing the friends who shared that fateful evening with Dan, I was struck by their youth. They were, like I imagine Dan is... a "normal" 14/15 year-old boy.

This tragic story was initially performed by a small group from the Oaklands Youth Theatre who were of a similar age to Daniel Nolan. I believe it can be performed between anyone from the age of 14 & 50. Whoever performs it must not lose sight of the fact that it tells a true story. Words should NOT be changed. Edits should NOT be made. Agreement was gained from all parties who contributed to the play on the understanding that this would be the version performed. **It is still an open investigation.** All performing groups must respect the willingness of the various families to allow their words to be used. I have slightly developed what I wrote in the introduction for **HARD TO SWALLOW**. It is equally pertinent for **DAN NOLAN – MISSING**.

It must at all times be remembered when reading or performing this play that the events portrayed are as close to the truth as memory will allow. The performers should not impersonate the real-life characters (it is unlikely that they will know them to be able to do so) but breathe into them a life that is a reasonable interpretation of the words in the book. Unless specifically instructed to do otherwise for a particular effect, the actors should avoid overstatement and veer towards underplaying. Trust the material. It is after all as near to possible the "real" thing.

The other thing to add here is to say that with these documentary plays there are often long speeches. It is crucial that these are not all static.

Introduction by Mark Wheeller

- **The National Missing Persons Helpline receives more than 100,000 calls every year!!!**
- **It helps to resolve 70% of the cases it works on.**
- **Therefore 30% remain tragically unresolved.**

These were the shocking statistics that confronted me when I approached a stand surrounded by "Dan Nolan MISSING" Posters outside Tesco's in April 2002.

I had originally seen posters announcing Dan's disappearance early in January while walking my dog. I continued to see them but as there had been nothing on the television about him I assumed that he had been found or perhaps that he was not missing after all. Somehow, as I came to realise that he was still missing it seemed like Dan's disappearance must be less important… less serious… or more likely to be resolved quickly. I could not understand it, so out of curiosity as to how a stall outside Tesco's could help, I approached to discover that they were trying to raise awareness. They had found it very difficult to get media coverage. As a parent (of three myself) I was shocked. I put myself in their position… how would I feel if my son or daughter went missing and I was not able to convey this fact to the public at large through the media. I realised I may be able to help.

To cut a long story short I offered to write a Dramatic reconstruction (also raising any other issues Dan's story might throw up). I approached four Oaklands Youth Theatre members to become committed to such a project in our own time. It was crucial to get "the show on the road" to help Dan's parents in their quest for more coverage sooner rather than later. First I had a period of research…

As I approached the Nolans' family home in Hamble, I saw posters plastered to every one of the thirty or forty trees and lamp-posts… the blow-ups of the posters constantly getting bigger as I drove into Hamble. It conveyed all too clearly the impression of a very loving family on a determined if not desperate search for a much-loved son.

One of the first things I saw as I went into the Nolans' house to do my first interview, was "that photo" I'd seen of Dan in the Missing Posters, in its original School Photo style frame… the way it was meant to be seen.

Dan Nolan – Missing

Whoever performs this play must not lose sight of the fact that it tells a true story. Words should not be changed. Edits should not be made. Agreement was gained from all parties who contributed to the play on the understanding that this would be the version performed.

It is still (at the time of publishing) an open investigation. All performing groups must respect the willingness of the various families to allow their words to be used in the way that they appear in this published text.

Enquiries regarding all rights associated with this play, including performing rights, should be addressed to:
Meg Davis, MBA Literary Agents Limited, 62 Grafton Way, London W1P 5LD.
Tel: 020 7387 2076   Fax: 020 7387 2042   E-mail: meg@mbalit.co.uk

A Prayer from the 'Service of Hope'

Where are you Dan?

The beautiful baby boy with big dark eyes

Who laid in my arms, when just a few hours old.

We watched you grow; a toddler, a little boy, and then onto school.

New friends, new interests, new skills, new sport; which you love so much.

All these things which helped you grow, to the maturing lad we all now know.

Working in your special quiet way towards your ambitions, goals and making dreams.

Where are you Dan?

Oh Lord we pray, please help him find his way back home to us, family and friends who love and miss him so.

Amen.

Nanny Bett (Dan's grandmother)
1st January 2003